Read for a
Better World

THERIZINOSAURUS
A First Look

JERI RANCH

GRL Consultant, Diane Craig, Certified Literacy Specialist

Lerner Publications ◆ Minneapolis

Educator Toolbox

Reading books is a great way for kids to express what they're interested in. Before reading this title, ask the reader these questions:

What do you think this book is about? Look at the cover for clues.

What do you already know about this dinosaur?

What do you want to learn about this dinosaur?

Let's Read Together

Encourage the reader to use the pictures to understand the text.

Point out when the reader successfully sounds out a word.

Praise the reader for recognizing sight words such as *had* and *was*.

TABLE OF CONTENTS

Therizinosaurus 4

Therizinosaurus

Therizinosaurus is a kind of dinosaur. It lived 70 million years ago.

Therizinosaurus
thay-ruh-zeen-oh-SOAR-us

The dinosaur
walked on two legs.
It was as tall as a giraffe.

giraffe

It had long arms.
It had sharp claws.
They were used to fight.

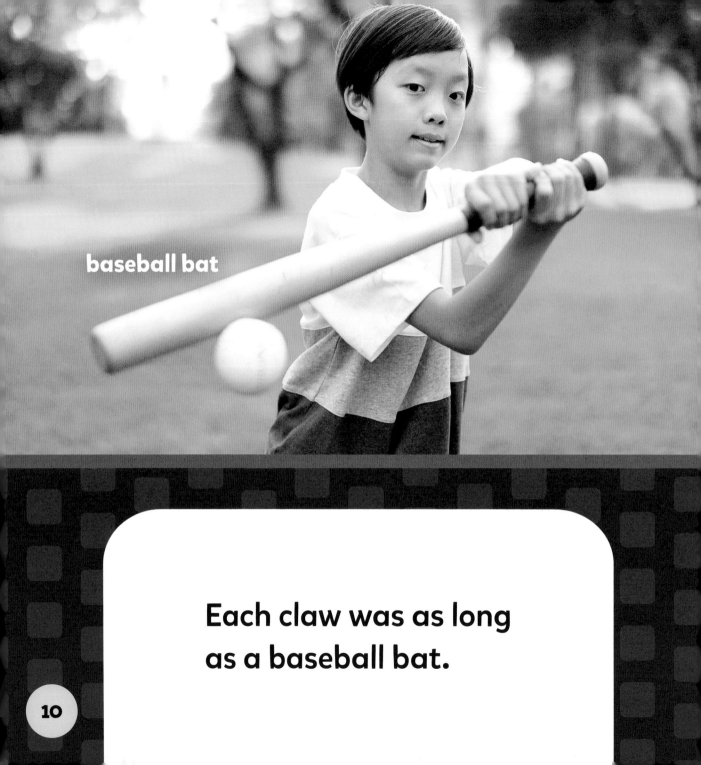

baseball bat

Each claw was as long
as a baseball bat.

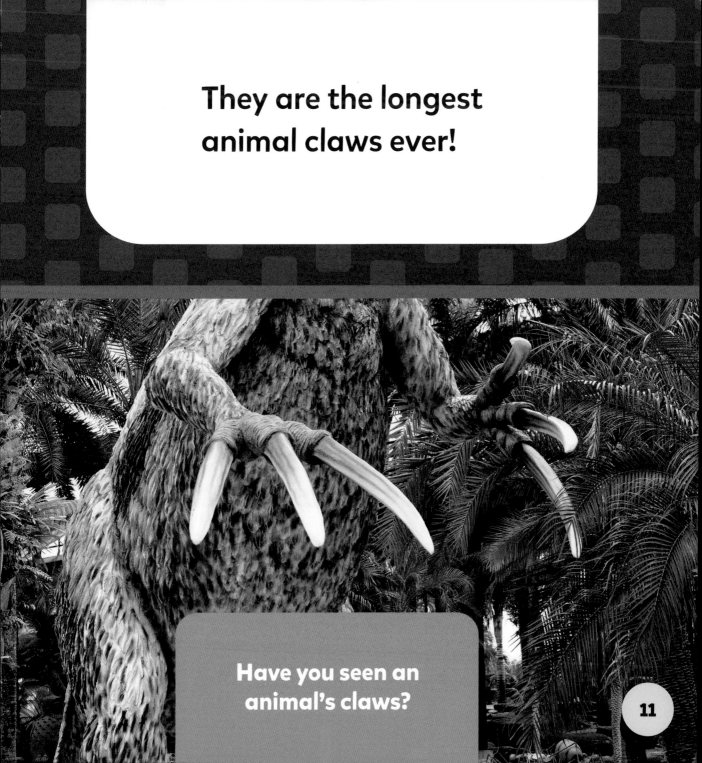

They are the longest animal claws ever!

Have you seen an animal's claws?

It mostly ate plants.
It may have eaten
small animals.

It had a small head.
It had a long neck.

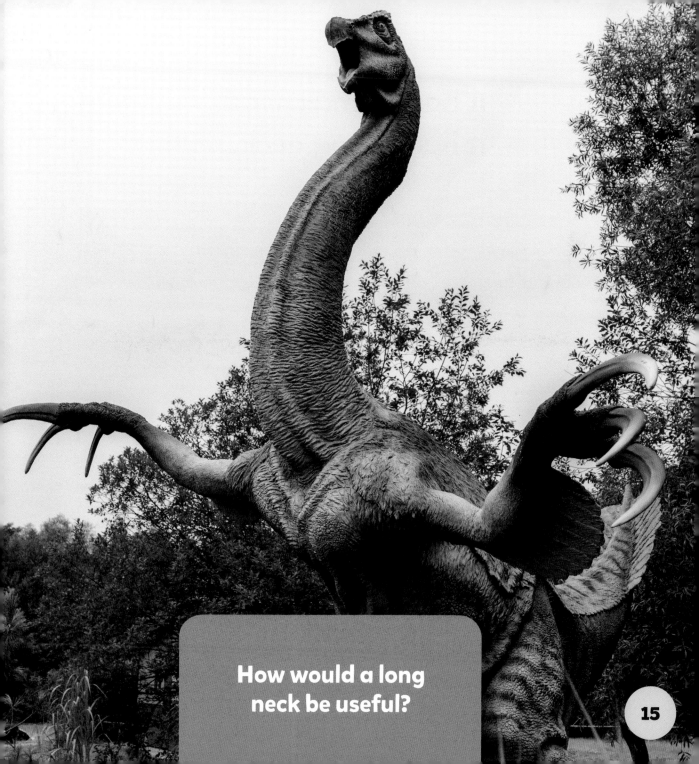

How would a long neck be useful?

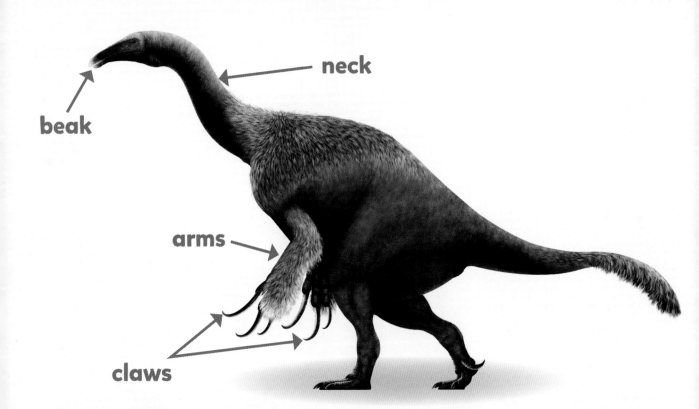

beak

neck

arms

claws

It had a beak.

It may have had feathers.

What other animals
have feathers?

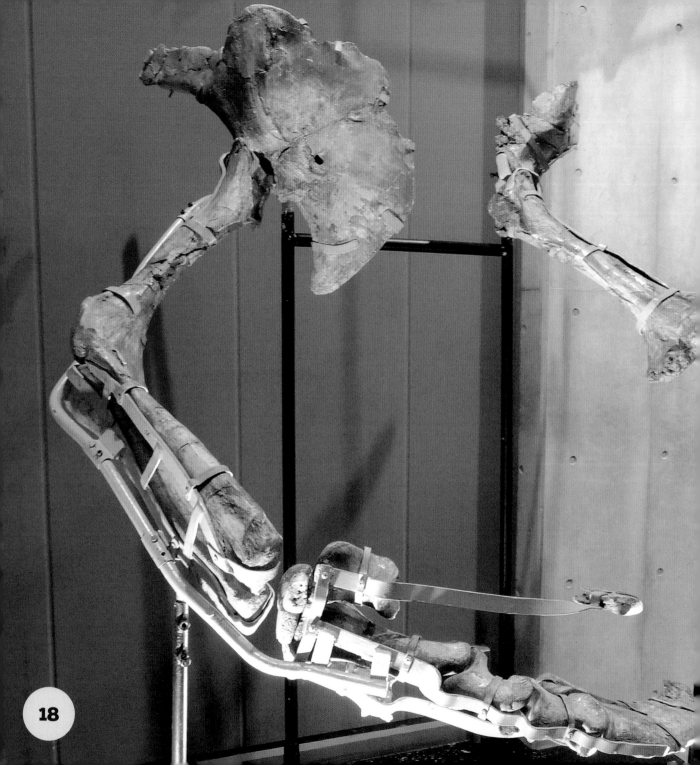

This dinosaur
is not alive today.
But people find its bones.

Bones teach us about this dinosaur.

You Connect!

What is something you like about this dinosaur?

What else looks like this dinosaur?

What other dinosaurs do you know about?

STEM Snapshot

Encourage students to think and ask questions like scientists. Ask the reader:

What is something you learned about this dinosaur?

What is something you noticed in the pictures of the dinosaur?

What is something you still don't know about this dinosaur?

Photo Glossary

beak

claws

feathers

giraffe

Learn More

Lundgren, Julie K. *Fossils and Dinosaurs*. New York: Crabtree Publishing Company, 2022.

McDonald, Jill. *Exploring Dinosaurs*. New York: Doubleday Books for Young Readers, 2023.

Walker, Alan. *Dinosaur Weapons*. New York: Crabtree Publishing Company, 2022.

Index

Photo Acknowledgments

The images in this book are used with the permission of: © Herschel Hoffmeyer/Shutterstock Images, pp. 4–5, 23 (feathers); © Karl Aage Isaksen/Shutterstock Images, pp. 6–7; © crbellette/iStockphoto, pp. 7, 23 (giraffe); © Catmando/Shutterstock Images, pp. 8–9; © real444/iStockphoto, p. 10; © Aleks49/Shutterstock Images, pp. 11, 17, 23 (claws); © dpa picture alliance/Alamy Photo, pp. 12–13; © Andrew Harker/Shutterstock Images, pp. 14, 23 (beak); © Lapis2380/Shutterstock Images, p. 15; © PaleoNeolitic/Wikimedia Commons, p. 16; © Yuya Tamai/Wikimedia Commons, pp. 18–19; © Kabacchi/Flickr, p. 20.

Cover Photograph: © Herschel Hoffmeyer/Shutterstock Images

Design Elements: © Mighty Media, Inc.

Lerner Publications Company
An imprint of Lerner Publishing Group, Inc.
241 First Avenue North
Minneapolis, MN 55401 USA

For reading levels and more information, look up this title at www.lernerbooks.com.

Main body text set in Mikado a Medium.
Typeface provided by Hannes von Doehren.

Library of Congress Cataloging-in-Publication Data

Names: Ranch, Jeri, author.
Title: Therizinosaurus : a first look / by Jeri Ranch.
Description: Minneapolis : Lerner Publications , [2024] | Series: Read about dinosaurs (Read for a better world) | Includes bibliographical references and index. | Audience: Ages 5–8 | Audience: Grades K–1 | Summary: "The Therizinosaurus had claws that were as long as baseball bats! With full-color images and easy-to-read text, readers can discover how the features of this dinosaur helped it survive"— Provided by publisher.
Identifiers: LCCN 2022039312 (print) | LCCN 2022039313 (ebook) | ISBN 9781728491370 (library binding) | ISBN 9798765603505 (paperback) | ISBN 9781728499345 (ebook)
Subjects: LCSH: Therizinosaurus—Juvenile literature. | Dinosaurs—Juvenile literature.
Classification: LCC QE862.S3 R35867 2024 (print) | LCC QE862.S3 (ebook) | DDC 567.913—dc23/eng/20220826

LC record available at https://lccn.loc.gov/2022039312
LC ebook record available at https://lccn.loc.gov/2022039313

Manufactured in the United States of America
3-1010774-51086-3/11/2024